SEYCHELLES 2016 HUMAN RIGHTS REPORT

EXECUTIVE SUMMARY

Seychelles is a multiparty republic governed by a president, Council of Ministers, and National Assembly. In December 2015 voters narrowly re-elected President James Michel of Parti Lepep. On September 27, President Michel announced he would resign effective October 16, passing the presidency to Vice President Danny Faure. The president and Parti Lepep, formerly the Seychelles People's Progressive Front, dominated the country through political patronage and control over government jobs, contracts, and resources. On September 11, the opposition coalition Seychellois Democratic Union won the majority of seats in Legislative Assembly elections, its first majority since establishing a multiparty system.

Civilian authorities maintained effective control over the security forces.

The most significant human rights problems were violence against women and children and denial of worker rights, particularly those of foreign workers.

Other human rights problems included police brutality; harassment of opposition politicians; prolonged pretrial detention; government restrictions on freedom of speech, association, and academic freedom; corruption; trafficking in persons; and forced labor.

The government took steps to punish officials who committed abuses, whether in the security services or elsewhere in the government, but impunity existed.

Section 1. Respect for the Integrity of the Person, Including Freedom from:

a. Arbitrary Deprivation of Life and other Unlawful or Politically Motivated Killings

There were no reports the government or its agents committed arbitrary or unlawful killings.

b. Disappearance

There were no reports of politically motivated disappearances.

c. Torture and Other Cruel, Inhuman, or Degrading Treatment or Punishment

The constitution and law prohibit such practices, but there were media reports police and National Drug Enforcement Agency officers beat and abused persons, including detainees, to force confessions. For example, on June 3, the newspaper *Seychelles Weekly* reported police severely beat Eddy Bibi, a resident of Ile Perseverance, when he resisted arrest. Bibi collapsed and was hospitalized the day after police arrested and jailed him. He was later released without charge.

Prison and Detention Center Conditions

Prison conditions were harsh due to overcrowding. Prisoners at Montagne Posee Prison alleged that a fellow inmate's death resulted from physical abuse.

Physical Conditions: Prison conditions and overcrowding in Montagne Posee Prison, the main prison, significantly improved during the year. On June 1, implementation of the Misuse of Drugs Act decriminalized possession of small amounts of cannabis. Consequently, authorities released approximately 160 prisoners because their convictions were overturned. No remand detainees, however, were released based on this change.

Authorities held pretrial detainees with convicted prisoners. Men and women were held in separate blocks in the same prison. Juvenile detainees and prisoners were held together with adult prisoners. On March 21, the newspaper *Seychelles Nation* reported the death of Montagne Posee Prison inmate Robert Banane. Prison officials initially stated that Banane died of a fall but later stated that he was shot. Sixty fellow inmates signed a letter sent to weekly newspaper *Le Seychellois Hebdo* stating Banane died while fighting for the right of inmates to be treated humanely.

Administration: An ombudsman may make recommendations to the National Assembly and the president to improve conditions for prisoners and detainees but had no authority to enforce such recommendations. Although the ombudsman is required to issue an annual report on inmate complaints and on investigations into human rights abuses and corruption, she did not do so for at least three years. Statistics on inmate complaints filed with the National Human Rights Commission were unavailable at year's end.

<u>Independent Monitoring</u>: The government generally permitted independent monitoring of prison conditions by local and international human rights groups. The UN Office on Drugs and Crime and three local nongovernmental organizations (NGOs) visited Montagne Posee Prison during the year. Several religious groups also visited the prison.

<u>Improvements</u>: Prison authorities initiated a methadone heroin replacement therapy program and a job placement program during the year. On January 13, a five-person holding center at the airport for undocumented migrants was completed.

d. Arbitrary Arrest or Detention

The constitution and law prohibit arbitrary arrest and detention, but the government did not always observe these prohibitions. Individuals posted allegations of arbitrary arrest and detention on social media sites. Following the December 2015 presidential elections, Mauritian lawyer Sanjay Bhuckory was detained and deported. According to government officials, Bhuckory misled immigration officials regarding the purpose of his visit, while government opponents claimed the deportation was politically motivated.

Role of the Police and Security Apparatus

The president controls the security apparatus, which includes the Seychelles People's Defense Forces (SPDF), Presidential Protection Unit, Coast Guard, and police. The police commissioner, who reports directly to the minister for home affairs, commands the unarmed police, the armed paramilitary Police Special Support Wing, and the Marine Police Unit, which together have primary responsibility for internal security. When necessary the SPDF assisted police on matters of internal security.

Security forces were effective, although impunity was a problem. Police brutality and corruption occurred, particularly the solicitation of bribes. On April 7, the independent daily newspaper *Today in Seychelles* reported two male police officers sexually assaulted a female colleague while on patrol. The two male officers were suspended, charged with sexual assault, released on bail, and had their passports confiscated. Their trial was pending at year's end.

Authorities rarely used the Enquiry Board, a police complaint office but rather established independent inquiry commissions to examine security force abuses.

Private attorneys generally filed complaints with police or published them in *Today in Seychelles* or in opposition party newspapers, such as *Seychelles Weekly* and *Le Seychellois Hebdo*. Although human rights were included as a core precept in officer training, the scope of such training was limited.

Arrest Procedures and Treatment of Detainees

The law requires warrants, except for persons arrested under the Misuse of Drugs Act, which allows police and National Drug Enforcement Agency officers to arrest and detain persons without a warrant. The law provides for detention without criminal charge for up to 14 days if authorized by court order. Persons arrested must be brought before a magistrate within 24 hours, with allowances for travel from distant islands. Police did not always respect this requirement. Authorities generally notified detainees of the charges against them and, unlike in previous years, generally granted family members prompt access to them. Detainees have the right to legal counsel, and indigents generally received free counsel. Courts allowed bail in most cases.

Arbitrary Arrest: Authorities committed unlawful detention and arbitrary or false arrest. For example, on September 1, *Today in Seychelles* reported police arrested political activist Bernard Sullivan for criminal trespass and held him for 24 hours. Sullivan was arrested in the course of researching an article about former president James Michel's property holdings. Although in an office open to the public, authorities accused Sullivan of "unlawful trespassing" but filed no charges against him.

Unlike in the previous years, there were no reports the government arbitrarily arrested demonstrators.

Pretrial Detention: The constitution provides that remand (pretrial) prisoners be released after six months of detention if their cases have not been heard, but prolonged pretrial detention was a problem. Prisoners sometimes waited more than three years for trial or sentencing due to case backlogs. Pretrial detainees made up approximately 16 percent of the prison population.

Detainee's Ability to Challenge Lawfulness of Detention before a Court: The constitution provides the right of persons arrested or detained to challenge the legal basis or arbitrary nature of their detention in court and seek compensation if found to have been unlawfully detained.

e. Denial of Fair Public Trial

The constitution and law provide for an independent judiciary, and the government generally respected judicial independence. Nevertheless, court processes were inefficient, and both civil and criminal court cases generally lasted years.

Supreme Court, appeals court, and magistrate court justices were either naturalized citizens or citizens of other Commonwealth countries. Judges generally were impartial. According to Freedom House, however, there were reports the executive branch interfered in the recruitment of foreign justices, who sometimes were hesitant to rule against the executive branch due to fear of losing their contracts; citizen judges, by contrast, had lifetime appointments. For example, on October 10, Supreme Court Judge Durai Karunakaran, a naturalized citizen, was suspended and under investigation for inability to conduct his duties; the opposition claimed his suspension was politically motivated because he made several rulings the government perceived to favor the opposition.

Authorities did not always respect court orders. On August 23, Supreme Court Judge Karunakaran threatened the electoral commissioner with contempt for refusing to obey his August 17 order to remove two political parties from the registry of political parties within 24 hours.

Trial Procedures

Defendants have the right to a fair, public trial; are considered innocent until proven guilty; and have the right to be present at their trials and to appeal. Defendants have the right to be informed promptly and in detail of the charges against them, with free interpretation as necessary from the first court appearance through all appeals. Only cases involving charges of murder or treason use juries. The constitution makes provision for defendants to present evidence and witnesses and to cross-examine witnesses in court. Defendants have the right to access government-held evidence, although responses to such requests often were delayed. The law provides the right of defendants to consult with an attorney of choice or to have one provided at public expense in a timely manner and to be provided adequate time and facilities to prepare a defense. Defendants have the right not to confess guilt, not to testify, or to enter a plea. The law extends these rights to all defendants.

Political Prisoners and Detainees

There were no reports of political prisoners or detainees.

Civil Judicial Procedures and Remedies

Individuals or organizations may seek civil remedies for human rights violations through domestic courts. For example, on January 12, *Today in Seychelles* reported the Supreme Court reversed a court ruling that forbade the Talma family of Praslin from developing their property in its entirety. In its finding, the court noted the right to own and enjoy property is a constitutional right.

Individuals may also appeal adverse domestic decisions to regional human rights bodies. For example, in 2014 *Today in Seychelles* reported Viral Dhanjee appealed to the African Court on Human and Peoples' Rights the rejection by the chief electoral officer of his nomination for the 2011 presidential elections. Because Seychelles was not party to the agreement establishing the court, it lacked jurisdiction, so Dhanjee sought relief from the UN Human Rights Committee. The case remained pending before the committee at year's end.

f. Arbitrary or Unlawful Interference with Privacy, Family, Home, or Correspondence

The constitution and law prohibit such actions, and the government generally respected these prohibitions. Nevertheless, there was widespread suspicion the government monitored private communications without legal process, and opposition activists claimed the government blocked access to their party websites and monitored their postings on social network sites.

Section 2. Respect for Civil Liberties, Including:

a. Freedom of Speech and Press

The constitution and law provide for freedom of speech and press, but the government did not always respect these rights. The government monopolized radio and television and used strict libel and slander laws to intimidate and harass independent journalists.

Freedom of Speech and Expression: Individuals who criticized the government publicly or privately sometimes suffered reprisals, such as harassment by police or the loss of jobs or contracts. For example, on January 27, Steve Narty, owner of the Island Sound Studio music-recording studio, claimed authorities ordered him to close his studio for recording a song favoring the political opposition.

Press and Media Freedoms: The government operated a daily newspaper. There were two privately owned newspapers, five political party weeklies, and the online news of the *Seychelles News Agency.* Unlike in the past, there were no reports the government discouraged companies from advertising in nongovernment-owned newspapers.

The government owned the only television station and two radio stations; there was one independent radio station. The law allows for independent radio and television but prohibits political parties and religious organizations from operating radio stations.

Censorship or Content Restrictions: The law allows the minister of information technology to prohibit the broadcast of any material believed to be against the "national interest" or "objectionable." The law also requires telecommunication companies to submit subscriber information to the government. The law was not enforced during the year, but journalists practiced self-censorship.

According to the Association of Media Practitioners of Seychelles, authorities denied some media houses access to certain government events and press conferences. During the elections, the opposition accused the Seychelles Broadcasting Corporation (SBC) of biased reporting and media coverage. On January 15, the four opposition presidential candidates and their supporters demanded that the SBC adhere to its constitutional mandate by giving equal coverage and treatment to all political sides.

Libel/Slander Laws: The law provides restrictions "for protecting the reputation, rights, and freedoms of private lives of persons" and "in the interest of defense, public safety, public order, public morality, or public health." As a result, civil lawsuits may be filed against print and broadcast journalists for alleged libel and slander. Social media sites may also be subject to libel lawsuits under this law.

Internet Freedom

Opposition activists claimed the government blocked access to their party websites and monitored their postings on social network sites. There also were reports the government monitored e-mails, internet chat rooms, and blogs. According to 2015

International Telecommunication Union statistics, 58 percent of the population used the internet.

Academic Freedom and Cultural Events

Political opposition activists claimed the government limited academic freedom by not allowing educators to reach senior positions in the academic bureaucracy without demonstrating at least nominal loyalty to Parti Lepep. The government controlled faculty appointments to the Polytechnic, the University of Seychelles, and boards of educational institutions. Opposition member Patrick Pillay stated that some students were denied admission to postsecondary educational institutions due to their parents' political affiliation.

b. Freedom of Peaceful Assembly and Association

Freedom of Assembly

The constitution and law provide for freedom of assembly, but the government did not always respect this right, and authorities had wide discretion to ban public gatherings and prosecute demonstrators, according to Freedom House.

In October 2015 the National Assembly replaced the Public Order Act with the Public Assembly Act, which requires organizers of gatherings of 10 or more persons to inform the police commissioner five working days prior to the date proposed for the planned gathering. The police commissioner may impose conditions or deny the right to assemble on security, morality, and public safety grounds. Unlike in previous years, authorities did not restrict the holding of lawful public opposition gatherings.

Freedom of Association

The constitution and law provide for freedom of association, but civil servants allegedly refrained from participating in opposition party activities due to fear of political reprisal. On September 15, *Today in Seychelles* reported that leader of the opposition Seychellois Democratic Union (LDS) Roger Mancienne called on the president to end the political victimization of civil servants who supported the LDS. Mancienne stated that they were harassed and threatened with termination. On October 11, the National Assembly approved a motion with bipartisan support to set up an antivictimization commission.

c. Freedom of Religion

See the Department of State's *International Religious Freedom Report* at www.state.gov/religiousfreedomreport/.

d. Freedom of Movement, Internally Displaced Persons, Protection of Refugees, and Stateless Persons

The constitution and law provide for freedom of internal movement, foreign travel, emigration, and repatriation. The government generally respected these rights.

Foreign Travel: The law allows the government to deny passports to any citizen if the minister of home affairs finds such denial "in the national interest."

Protection of Refugees

Access to Asylum: The law does not provide for the granting of asylum or refugee status, and the government has not established a system for providing protection to refugees. Nevertheless, the country cooperated with the UN High Commissioner for Refugees, which monitored and assisted refugees in the country through a memorandum of understanding with the UN Development Program. For example, in 2013 Sakher El Materi, the son-in-law of former Tunisian president Ben Ali, was granted political temporary residence on the ground he would not receive a fair trial if sent back to Tunisia. El Materi remained in the country at year's end.

Section 3. Freedom to Participate in the Political Process

The constitution provides citizens the ability to choose their government through free and fair periodic elections held by secret ballot and based on universal and equal suffrage.

Elections and Political Participation

Recent Elections: In December 2015 President Michel was re-elected to a third term by 193 votes in the country's first-ever runoff election. Neither Michel nor runner-up Wavel Ramkalawan, leader of the opposition alliance Seychelles National Party, received the required 50 percent plus one vote to win in the first round of elections held between December 3 and 5. International observers from the Southern African Development Community and the African Union, who had not determined whether the elections were free and fair by year's end, criticized voter intimidation and vote buying.

The opposition petitioned the Constitutional Court to overturn the elections based on election irregularities including vote buying. On May 31, the Constitutional Court ruled that, although there were irregularities, they were not significant enough to overturn the elections.

On September 8-10, National Assembly elections were held. An opposition alliance comprising the Seychelles National Party, the Lalyans Seselwa party, the Seychelles Party for Social Justice and Democracy, and supporters of independent presidential candidate Phillipe Boulle, won 15 seats in the 33-seat assembly, while the Parti Lepep won 10 seats. The remaining seats were allocated on a proportional basis, with the alliance and Parti Lepep each receiving four additional seats. International and domestic observers qualified the election as transparent, fair, and peaceful but refrained from calling it free due to the lack of credibility of the election management body, the Seychelles Electoral Commission.

Political Parties and Political Participation: Parti Lepep assumed power in a 1977 coup and continued to dominate the country through a pervasive system of political patronage and control over government jobs, contracts, and resources. Opposition parties claimed they operated under restrictions and subject to outside interference. Some opposition party members claimed they lost their government jobs because of their political affiliation and were at a disadvantage when applying for government licenses and loans.

On September 27, the first day of the National Assembly session, President Michel announced his resignation, passing the presidency to Vice President Danny Faure of Parti Lepep, effective October 16.

Participation of Women and Minorities: There are no laws or practices that prevent women from fully engaging in politics. Following the September National Assembly elections, women held seven seats compared with 14 seats they held in the previous assembly.

Section 4. Corruption and Lack of Transparency in Government

The law provides criminal penalties for conviction of official corruption, but the government did not always implement the law effectively, and officials sometimes

engaged in corrupt practices with impunity. The World Bank's most recent
Worldwide Governance Indicators reflected corruption was a problem.

Financial Disclosure: The law requires senior public servants and board members
to declare their assets in a sealed envelope deposited in the Seychelles Central
Bank's vault. The declaration of assets may be disclosed if a legal challenge is
filed. The law was not always enforced.

Public Access to Information: There are laws allowing public access to
government information, but the government did not comply with them. Citizens
generally had no access to such information.

Section 5. Governmental Attitude Regarding International and Nongovernmental Investigation of Alleged Violations of Human Rights

Government officials generally were cooperative and responsive to the views of
international NGOs. With the exception of Friends of Prison--which provided a
platform for prisoners' families to register their concerns--the government was less
cooperative with local NGOs, which it perceived as aligned with the opposition.

Government Human Rights Bodies: The National Human Rights Commission,
which generally operated without government or party interference, lacked
adequate resources and was rarely used due to a public perception it was inefficient
and aligned with the government.

Section 6. Discrimination, Societal Abuses, and Trafficking in Persons

Women

Rape and Domestic Violence: Rape, spousal rape, and domestic abuse are criminal
offenses for which conviction is punishable by a maximum of 20 years'
imprisonment. Nevertheless, rape was a problem, and the government did not
enforce the law effectively. Most victims did not report rape due to fear of reprisal
or social stigma. As of September 1, authorities received only five reports of rape.
Only 13 other cases of sexual assault were prosecuted, and none resulted in
conviction.

Domestic violence against women was a problem and underreported. Police rarely
responded to domestic disputes, although media continued to draw attention to the
problem. Police maintained a specialized unit, the Family Squad, to address

domestic violence and other family problems. The unit was underfunded and ineffective. Judicial authorities often dismissed the few cases that reached a prosecutor. In the cases that resulted in conviction, judges generally handed down light sentences. As of September 1, of 27 reported cases of domestic violence, 11 were prosecuted.

The Social Affairs Division of the Ministry of Health and Social Affairs and NGOs, provided counseling services to victims of rape and domestic violence. The ministry's Gender Secretariat conducted various outreach campaigns to end gender-based violence.

Sexual Harassment: The law prohibits sexual harassment, but enforcement was rare. The penal code provides no penalty for sexual harassment, although the court may order a person accused of such conduct to "keep a bond of peace," which allows the court to assess a fine if the harasser fails to cease the harassment.

Reproductive Rights: Couples and individuals have the right to decide freely and responsibly the number, spacing, and timing of their children and to have access to the information and means to do so, free from discrimination, coercion, or violence. Health clinics and local NGOs operated freely in disseminating information on family planning under the guidance of the Ministry of Health. The government provided free childbirth services including doctors, nurses, and midwives for delivery and for prenatal and postnatal care. Men and women had equal access to diagnosis and treatment for sexually transmitted infections. There were no legal, social, cultural, or other barriers to accessing these services.

Discrimination: The law provides for the same legal status and rights for women as for men, and the society is largely matriarchal. While unwed mothers were the societal norm, the law requires fathers to support their children. In June 2015 the Employment Act was amended to provide fathers with five days of paternity leave upon the birth of a child. There was no officially sanctioned discrimination in employment, and women were well represented in both the public and private sectors.

There was no economic discrimination against women in employment, access to credit, equal pay for equal work, or owning or managing a business. Inheritance laws do not discriminate against women.

Children

<u>Birth Registration</u>: Citizenship is derived by birth in the country or from parents, and births generally were registered immediately.

<u>Child Abuse</u>: Although the law prohibits physical abuse of children, child abuse was a problem. According to government social workers, perpetrators of child sexual abuse often were stepfathers and other family members. According to the NGO Women in Action and Solidarity Organization, most rapes of girls under age 15 went unreported due to fear of reprisal or social stigma. Authorities prosecuted several child abuse cases in court. The strongest public advocate for young victims was a semiautonomous agency, the National Council for Children.

<u>Early and Forced Marriage</u>: The minimum age for marriage is 15 years for girls with parental consent and 18 years for boys. Child marriage was not a significant problem.

<u>Sexual Exploitation of Children</u>: The law criminalizes the prostitution and sexual exploitation of children and specifically prohibits the procurement, recruitment, or exploitation of children under age 18 for the purpose of prostitution. The law also prohibits the procurement or detainment of any child against his or her will with the intent to engage in sexual conduct or for the purpose of prostitution. The law provides for a minimum 14 years' imprisonment for the first conviction of sexual assault on a person under age 15, and 28 years' imprisonment for a second conviction. The 2014 Prohibition of Trafficking in Persons Act prescribes penalties of up to 25 years' imprisonment for conviction of child trafficking.

Sexual exploitation of children was a problem. There were credible reports of commercial sexual exploitation of children, and many of the cases went unreported. Few complaints were filed with police, and no abusers were prosecuted during the year. No cases of child pornography, which is illegal, were reported during the year.

<u>International Child Abductions</u>: The country is a party to the 1980 Hague Convention on the Civil Aspects of International Child Abduction. See the Department of State's *Annual Report on International Parental Child Abduction* at <u>travel.state.gov/content/childabduction/en/legal/compliance.html</u>.

Anti-Semitism

The Jewish community numbered fewer than 10 persons. There were no reports of anti-Semitic acts.

Trafficking in Persons

See the Department of State's *Trafficking in Persons Report* at
www.state.gov/j/tip/rls/tiprpt/.

Persons with Disabilities

Although the constitution and law provide for the right of persons with disabilities
to special protection, including reasonable provisions for improving quality of life,
no laws provide for access to public buildings, transportation, or government
services, and the government did not provide such services. There was
discrimination against persons with disabilities. For example, there were reports
some employers did not pay their employees with disabilities if the latter were
already receiving disability social aid (see section 7.d.). Most children with
disabilities were segregated in specialized schools. The National Council for the
Disabled, a government agency under the Ministry of Health and Social Affairs,
developed work placement programs for persons with disabilities, although few
employment opportunities existed.

Acts of Violence, Discrimination, and Other Abuses Based on Sexual Orientation and Gender Identity

On May 18, consensual same-sex activity between men was decriminalized. There
were few reports of discrimination against lesbian, gay, bisexual, transgender, and
intersex (LGBTI) persons, although LGBTI activists reported social stigma
prevented incidents from being pursued. On July 18, *Today in Seychelles* carried a
local LGBTI activist's opinion editorial that described the barriers LGBTI persons
faced in obtaining public housing and access to health care. On June 30,
authorities registered a local NGO formed to advocate for the rights of LGBTI
persons that submitted its registration documents in September 2015; the normal
registration approval process ordinarily took 10 to 14 days.

HIV and AIDS Social Stigma

There were no reports of violence or discrimination against persons with
HIV/AIDS. Nevertheless, the government has informal policies that require a
foreign citizen marrying a Seychellois to undergo an HIV test. If the test is
positive, the couple is not permitted to marry in the country. On April 29, a
national policy on HIV/AIDS in the workplace was initiated that provides for core

guidelines and responses for HIV/AIDS in the workplace including nondiscriminatory employment practices.

Section 7. Worker Rights

a. Freedom of Association and the Right to Collective Bargaining

The law allows all workers, excluding police, military, prison, and firefighting personnel, to form and join independent unions and to bargain collectively. The law confers on the registrar discretionary powers to refuse registration of unions. Strikes are illegal unless arbitration procedures are first exhausted. The legislation requires that two-thirds of union members vote for a strike in a meeting specifically called to discuss the strike and provides the government with the right to call for a 60-day cooling off period before a strike starts. The law allows the minister of employment and human resources development to declare a strike unlawful if its continuance would endanger, among other things, "public order or the national economy." Anyone found guilty of calling for an illegal strike may be fined 5,000 rupees ($370) and imprisoned for up to six months.

Between 15 and 20 percent of the workforce was unionized. The law prohibits antiunion discrimination but is silent regarding the rights of foreign or migrant workers to join a union. The government has the right to review and approve all collective bargaining agreements in the public and private sectors. The law also imposes compulsory arbitration in all cases where negotiating parties do not reach an agreement through collective bargaining. In the Seychelles International Trade Zone (SITZ), the country's export processing zone, the government did not require adherence to all labor, property, tax, business, or immigration laws. The Seychelles Trade Zone Act supersedes many legal provisions of the labor, property, tax, business, and immigration laws. The Employment Tribunal handles employment disputes for private-sector employees. The Public Services Appeals Board handles employment disputes for public-sector employees, and the Financial Services Agency deals with employment disputes of workers in the SITZ. The law authorizes the Ministry of Employment and Human Resources Development to establish and enforce employment terms, conditions, and benefits, and workers frequently obtained recourse against their employers through the ministry or the Employment Tribunal.

The government did not effectively enforce applicable laws. Penalties came in the form of fines and were often inadequate to deter violations. Cases involving citizens were often subject to lengthy delays and appeals, while foreigners were often deported.

The government did not always respect the right to participate in union activities and collective bargaining. The International Labor Organization continued to report insufficient protection against acts of interference and restrictions on collective bargaining. It urged the government to review provisions of the Industrial Relations Act concerning trade union registration and the right to strike. Although the law prohibits antiunion discrimination, there were unofficial reports that such discrimination occurred. The law allows employers or their organizations to interfere by promoting the establishment of worker organizations under their control. Collective bargaining rarely occurred.

b. Prohibition of Forced or Compulsory Labor

The law prohibits all forms of forced or compulsory labor, but government enforcement was ineffective. Penalties for violations included imprisonment of up to 14 years, which was inadequate to deter violations. Resources, inspections, and remediation were also inadequate. There were credible reports that forced labor occurred in the fishing and construction sectors, where most of the country's nearly 19,000 migrants worked; however, no cases of forced labor were prosecuted.

See also the Department of State's *Trafficking in Persons Report* at www.state.gov/j/tip/rls/tiprpt/.

c. Prohibition of Child Labor and Minimum Age for Employment

The law states the minimum age for employment is 15 years, "subject to exceptions for children who are employed part time in light work prescribed by law without harm to their health, morals, or education." The law does not establish a minimum age for hazardous work but does provide for a list of hazardous work that children under 15 are prohibited from doing.

The government generally enforced the laws, and the Ministry of Employment and Human Resources Development effectively enforced child labor laws. The penalty for employing a child under age 15 was a fine of 6,000 rupees ($444), which was sufficient to deter violations. The ministry employed 13 labor inspectors, who handled such complaints within its general budget and staffing, and did not report any case requiring investigation.

See the Department of Labor's *Findings on the Worst Forms of Child Labor* at
www.dol.gov/ilab/reports/child-labor/findings/.

d. Discrimination with Respect to Employment and Occupation

Labor laws and regulations prohibit discrimination regarding race, sex, religion,
gender, political opinion, national origin or citizenship, social origin, disability,
language, sexual orientation or gender identity, HIV-positive status or other
communicable diseases, or social status. It does not address age or color.

The government effectively enforced these laws and regulations. Penalties came in
the form of fines and were sufficient to deter violations.

Employment discrimination generally did not occur in practice. There were
reports some employers did not pay their employees with disabilities if the latter
were already receiving disability social aid (see section 6). Women received equal
pay for equal work, as well as equal access to credit, business ownership, and
management positions.

e. Acceptable Conditions of Work

In the public sector, which employed more than 50 percent of the labor force, the
government set mandatory wage rates for employees. The Ministry of Finance,
Trade, and the Blue Economy (activities linked to the exploitation of marine
resources) determined the minimum wage of 33.30 rupees ($ 2.46) per hour for all
workers. Employers, however, generally set wages through individual agreements
with the employee. According to a 2013 National Bureau of Statistics
Seychelles/World Bank report, *Poverty Profile of the Republic of the Seychelles*,
the monthly poverty income level was 3,945 rupees ($327) per adult.

The legal maximum workweek varied from 45 to 55 hours, depending on the
economic sector. Regulations entitled each full-time worker to a one-hour break
per day and a minimum of 21 days of paid annual leave, including paid annual
holidays. Regulations permitted overtime up to 60 additional hours per month.
The law requires premium pay for overtime work.

The Ministry of Health sets comprehensive occupational health and safety
regulations, which are current and appropriate for the main industries. The law
allows citizen workers to remove themselves from dangerous or unhealthy work
situations, to report the employer to the Health and Safety Commission of the

Department of Employment, and to seek compensation without jeopardizing their employment. The law provides for the protection of foreign workers.

The government generally supported these standards but did not effectively enforce them in all sectors. Resources, inspections, and remediation were inadequate. Penalties for violations included a fine of 10,000 rupees ($740) plus additional daily fines for noncompliance, as detailed in the Occupational Safety and Health Decree. These penalties were not sufficient to deter violations.

The Ministry of Health and Social Affairs and the Ministry for Employment are responsible for visiting and inspecting work sites and workers accommodation. There were 13 safety and health inspectors; these were insufficient to enforce compliance.

Foreign workers, primarily employed in the construction and commercial fishing sectors, did not always enjoy the same legal protections as citizens. Companies in the SITZ sometimes paid foreign workers lower wages, delayed payment of their salaries, forced them to work longer hours, and provided them with inadequate housing, resulting in substandard conditions.

As of September 1, there were 41 occupational accidents reported, which occurred most frequently in the hotel and restaurant, transport, and storage industries.

Notes

Notes